Stories from the Quran
Book 1

The Story of the Creation
&
Noah *(Nuh)* and the Ark

Written by
Noura Durkee
Illustrated by
Shehraz Afzal

The Story of The Creation

In the beginning there was only God.

God was all alone.

Then He decided to make everything.

He said: **"BE!"**

And everything was made.

God made light from dark.

From the light He made angels

and in the dark He placed stars.

Millions of them!

Then He made galaxies and comets,

planets and the Milky Way.

Then God made Earth.

On Earth, God made the sky,

to hold the water and the air.

From the sky came rain

And rain made life.

Then God made tall mountains,

volcanoes of fire

and deep dark valleys.

On Earth, God made every kind of plant and animal.

From the trees and plants came forests

and gardens of fruit and flowers.

Yellow and red. Green and orange.

Big and small. Round and thin.

In the forests lived the animals, insects and birds.

And in the seas lived the fish.

Whales and elephants and gorillas.

Mice **and** ladybirds **and** ants.

They were all *swimming, crawling,*

flying, climbing, creeping.

Then God made Man

to take care of the forests, trees and plants,

the animals, birds, fish and insects.

Man's name was Adam.

And God looks over *all* of His Creation

***all* the time.**

He never *ever* naps or sleeps.

Noah *(Nuh)* and the Ark

God told Noah to build a big boat.

First Noah planted some trees.

Then he chopped the wood.

Then he began to build the boat.

It was very big.

Some people laughed at Noah.

They thought he was crazy.

But Noah was a Prophet.

When the boat was built, God said:

"Tell the good people to get on board.

And all the animals, two by two."

Monkeys, parrots and pandas.

Crocodiles and turtles.

Giraffes, rhinos and elephants.

Lions and tigers.

The animals all came running.

They all hurried into the boat.

Soon, it began to rain and rain.

All the land was covered with water.

Even the mountains.

Nothing was there but the big boat,

bobbing up and down!

After a long time, the rain stopped.

Noah sent a dove to find land.

It came back with a leaf from a tree.

Land was near!

 *BUMP!*

The boat landed on top of a mountain!

The good people were safe.

So were the animals.

Copyright © Hood Hood Books 1998
Reprinted 2006

Hood Hood Books
39 Thurloe Street,
London SW7 2LQ

Tel: 44 20 7584 7878
Fax: 44 20 7225 0386
Web-Site: www.hoodhood.com
E-Mail: info@hoodhood.com

British Library Cataloguing–in–Publication Data
A catalogue record for this book is available from the British Library

ISBN 1 900251 50 7

No part of this book may be reproduced
in any form without permission of the publishers.
All rights reserved.

Origination by: *Fine Line Graphics Ltd*, London

PUBLISHER'S NOTE

According to the *hadith* (saying) of the Prophet Muhammad, peace be upon him, it is traditional practice not to depict God's Angels, Messengers and Prophets in any form of visual representation. There are no such depictions in this book.